# Product Engineering In the Cloud

AJITH JOSEPH

"There is no friend as loyal as a book"
— Ernest Hemingway

# DEDICATION

All that is good, all that is perfect, is given us from above; it comes down from the Father of all light; with him there is no such thing as alteration, no shadow caused by change.
James 1- 17.

I dedicate this book to my daughter Joanna and son Joackim!

# ABOUT THIS BOOK

Technology landscape has already reached the startups-land which means that there is a startup or there will be a startup out there to automate everything that was once hardware to now software; and if you have an idea as well and you want to see it in action in the cloud, this book is for you.

If you have a proof of concept that runs locally on your developer laptop and you are clueless on how to go about on deploying it to cloud, this book is for you.

The book facilitate in setting up a cloud based environment at enterprise level or at direct-to-customer level through 2 of the world's largest cloud providers – Amazon Web Services® and Red Hat OpenShift®.

The book also gives a hint in dockerizing your application. You can also read about setting up on-demand scaling for a single page web-scale multi tenant application.

Disclaimer: The opinions expressed in this book are my own and do not necessarily represent those of my current or past employers.

## Who this book is for:

This book is for entrepreneurs or for the following categories of professionals:

- This book is for those who walk the walk of IT and talk the talk of business.

That implies this book is for enterprise architects (EA) or enterprise IT architects (EITA). This book will help them lift-and-shift a product that runs on premises or on local development environments as proof of concepts to cloud. This book will also help you give your fresh business ideas a concrete cloud shell.

- This book is for those who solve the jig-saw puzzles of dev-ops and infrastructure when dealing with an enterprise level or even a non-enterprise level application.

That implies this book is for devops discipline as well. This book will help a devops architect or a cloud architect to visualize a product that actually runs in the cloud. However this book neither get into the details of coding and development nor help you decide what architecture to follow, as in service oriented versus or as in micro services. But this book will surely help you in setting up, scaling up and help you continuously integrate and continuously deploy and deliver your product in the cloud.

One of the important factors I have considered while working on this book is that the reader should be able to read through this book in about 2 hours (considering a fast-average reader) and will be able to prototype/engineer right after reading this guide.

# FOREWORD

As CTO of Intellect SEEC, I worked with Ajith where he played a key role in turning our "old school" physical dev ops infrastructure to true Cloud based Engineering. This was a wholesale change in technology, people and process, tantamount to changing a jet engine in mid flight (and making it go faster using less fuel). The demands on him from the application development team alone were high. This was way more than just re-platforming and choosing a Cloud provider, this was going to result in a total business model change.

As Marc Andreessen says, "Software is eating the world", for DevOps this means what was once infrastructure is now software. This gives you a level of flexibility to creating your Product Engineering in the Cloud environment. However with infinite flexibility is infinite choice. This is important as in most things; technology has a lot of choices and with multiple overlapping options in every area. Building the ecosystem that is best for you is more about how you "plumb" these tools together. This is what I believe Ajith will help you achieve. Ajith has taken this practitioners approach and created a "playbook" with Product Engineering in the Cloud for what he did and what he learnt, taking the journey from what are the Cloud is (yes Cloud is way more than just deploying on a Cloud platform) to managing containers, disaster recovery, monitoring, continuous integration etc.. He mixes in "Fun Facts" and anecdotes with some historical context to the technology and what our team actually did in situations.

I hope you enjoy reading about Ajith's innovative approach to Cloud engineering and wish you all the best in setting up your own Product Engineering in the Cloud.

- Lakshan Desilva
  Partner & Chief Technology Officer
  Intellect SEEC

About Lakshan: He is currently leading the transformation of Intellect SEEC products to an AI based and cloud first portfolio. He is bringing in exponential technology that will define the next 10 years into the Intellect SEEC products. His current projects revolve around AI and Blockchain.

# CONTENTS

# ACKNOWLEDGMENTS

Thanksgiving is a natural instinct of praising God and I thank Holy Spirit for the seeds of thoughts for writing this book. I would like to thank the love of my life, Nisha and the apple of my eye, my daughter Joanna and my son, our little Santa, Joackim, for letting me spend my weekends for the writing. They get me going all the time no matter what difficulty I face. I also thank my parents and my brother for their endless support.

From professional front, there are a lot of people who I would like to thank and some of the names that can never be excluded are Pramod Kusuma, Lakshan De Silva, Mahesh M, Nilesh Dambe, Ravi Koka, Mohanrao LV and Piyush Kumar Nahata. Without their leadership I would not have had a chance to learn so much that shapes up what I am today. I would also like to underline a special thanks to Intellect Design Chairman, Arun Jain; Intellect SEEC CEO, Pranav Pasricha and Lakshan De Silva, Intellect SEEC CTO for their exemplary leadership practices.

There are many others with whom I had knowledge handshakes. Limiting the names due to space limitations does not mean that they are not remembered and acknowledged.

Thank you all!

# 1

## INTIRODUCTION TO CLOUD BASED APPLICATIONS

A cloud based application is generally a duck or a rabbit. It just depends on how you look at it. Let us take a deep dive into the topic and then you may be able to decide that for yourself.

With startup landscape growing huge again, cloud computing is a de facto standard for infrastructure engineering.

**Basics of cloud computing:**

Cloud computing is an agile way of provisioning and re-provisioning technological infrastructure resources on an on-demand basis. Cloud computing environments can be set up on an on-premise data center or on a 3rd party data center.

When it is setup on an on-premise data center, it is generally termed as private cloud. And when it is setup on a 3<sup>rd</sup> party data center, it is generally termed as public cloud. When it is setup on a mix of both on-premises and 3<sup>rd</sup> party data center, it is termed as hybrid cloud.

Apart from the above 3 categorizations, there is a 4<sup>th</sup> one named as community cloud. Community cloud can otherwise be visualized as the subset of public cloud that is tailored to a specific business vertical. In community cloud, infrastructure is mutually shared between many organizations that belong to a particular community, i.e. banks and insurance careers for example.

Interestingly there is a new 5<sup>th</sup> category named 'thin cloud' and a good example of it is the increasingly popular 'blockchain'.

Blockchain is a hot technology in the tech finance world that is considered as the next generation transactional applications that streamlines business process by establishing trust, accountability and transparency. It can also be considered as a programmable ledger. Programmable ledger is a design pattern made famous by bitcoin, but its uses go far beyond. For your reference, Bitcoin is an open source form of peer to peer or business to business money.

## Service Model:

Cloud computing adopts the American way of self-servicing in IT infrastructure world. A cloud computing provider offers a self servicing stack that has one or more of the following components.

a) Infrastructure as a Service (IaaS)
b) Platform as a Service (PaaS)
c) Software as a Service (SaaS)

## Infrastructure as a Service (IaaS):

One of the most basic cloud model where cloud providing company offers a pay-as-you-go hardware is known as Infrastructure as a Service. The hardware can actually be a bare metal physical server, a virtualized server – a Virtual Machine (VM), a storage device, a load balancing hardware, a network device such as a router and switches or a VPN device.

For example, this is the service with which you can provision an on-demand Linux flavor or Windows flavor Virtual Machine (VM) on an Amazon Web Services (AWS) cloud subscription.

Major IaaS providers include Amazon Web Services, Windows Azure, Rackspace, Digital Ocean, Google Compute Engine, Joyent, IBM SoftLayer, Red Hat Enterprise Linux Open Stack

Platform and Collabnet CloudForge.

Please note that Mac OS X server VMs are not available with the major player AWS at the time of writing this book. Stack Overflow has a question-answer thread on Mac OS X cloud services.

URL:   http://bit.ly/stackoverflow-1

Note:   All URLs bookmarked in this book are shortened using bit.ly. It is a bookmarking / URL shortening utility launched by Bitly, Inc.

Some of the Mac cloud offerings are granulated here for reference. Please note that credibility of these services is not validated by the author:

URL:   http://bit.ly/mac-cloud-1
       http://bit.ly/mac-cloud-2
       http://bit.ly/mac-cloud-3
       http://bit.ly/mac-cloud-4

In this book, I will walk through product engineering on AWS IaaS and on Red Hat OpenShift Online PaaS. Mac OS X is out of scope for this book.

**Platform as a Service (PaaS):**

Platform-as-a-Service (PaaS) is a cloud practice that allows developers to use out of the box web server/ application server/ database server infrastructure. PaaS takes care of the entire sysadmin life cycle and developers can just focus on coding and configurations. The pain of provisioning, managing and scaling are left out to the PaaS provider. Red Hat OpenShift is a pioneer in this area.

## Software as a Service (SaaS):

Software as a Service is generally a product (web based/mobile based) offered online and would not require nothing more than a web browser to run. It runs as a cloud service but not generally need to be hosted on a cloud platform (IaaS or PaaS). In fact, Salesforce, Inc. a $45 billion cloud based company founded in 1999 is often the best example of an enterprise SaaS and their underlying infrastructure is still not on cloud at the writing of this book. Another great example of a consumer application is Gmail (email client software as a service from Google).

## Deployment Model:

When planning on a cloud based product, there are many areas that need brainstorming, especially if a muti-tenant is on the plans. Following are some of the deployment models to consider.

## Private Cloud:

Private cloud is generally for a single organization and if you already have a physical foot print, i.e., a data center available, it is a good idea to set it up as a private cloud, provided deployments are done right. You have to consider the enterprise work load on a use case by use case basis to arrive at the decision of implementing private cloud. Otherwise it can be catastrophic, especially with applications with unknown traffic patterns. One major downside to this model is that you have to buy physical resources (or reuse if you already own resources), build it using a tool such as Open Stack, Appistry, Gigaspaces, Ubuntu Cloud or Oracle Nimbula or any such tool, and finally manage the cloud by yourself. It is generally single tenant (from cloud hosting perspective) since you are the only customer on board unless you are reselling it as a public/closed cloud offering.

## Public Cloud:

Public cloud is the true representation of cloud hosting. In a public cloud hosting, cloud resources are delivered over Internet which is open for public usage. Research and advisory consultancies such as International Data Corporation (IDC), Forrester, Gartner, Ovum, Wikibon and others have published reports of the usage of various deployment models and public cloud model stands out at the top. Forbes magazine states that the majority (57%) of enterprise Infrastructure as a Service customer uses AWS today, as of early 2016.

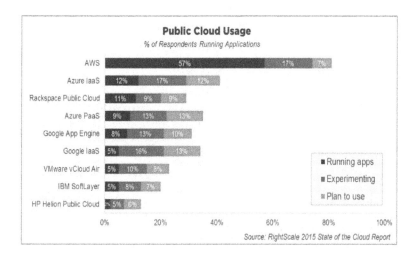

**Figure 1.1: Public Cloud Market Share - 2015**

## Hybrid Cloud:

When a composition of two or more classification of cloud models is made, it's essentially known as a Hybrid Cloud model. That means when a private, public or community cloud models are bound together and when it offers multiple deployment models, it can be called as hybrid cloud. Hybrid cloud offers the ability to connect collocation. It also helps in managing dedicated services with cloud resources. The 3$^{rd}$ party tools such as Open Stack as specified in 'Private Cloud' section above can be used to build a hybrid cloud model.

## Community Cloud:

Community cloud as specified above shares infrastructure among organizations. An example is, International Game Technology, which is a vendor of computerized game technology. They recently launched its community cloud version named as IGT Cloud and it is aimed specifically at gaming companies. Using the App Logic cloud computing platform from CA Technologies, IGT cloud provides cloud-based Software as a Service offerings for casinos to better manage their games.

**Other deployment models:**

a) Distributed cloud – This classification of cloud model is a glued form of distributed data centers in different locations connected as a homogeneous network or hub service. Example would be FAH (Folding@home), a protein folding platform authored by Prof. Vijay Pande of Stanford University, California.
b) Intercloud – Aims at interoperability between public cloud providers.
c) Multicloud – Choice of using multiple cloud providers for a single product is a good use case of Multicloud.

**Fun facts:**

We saw that cloud is the best example for self servicing. Self service is the practice of serving oneself, usually when purchasing items. It was the brainchild of American businessman Clarence Saunders. Self servicing was first implemented by piggly wiggly® a grocery shop based out of Memphis, Tennessee.

## Major cloud providers:

We are going to cover only AWS (IaaS) and Red Hat Open Shift (PaaS) in this book to do our product engineering in the cloud learning/exercise.

## AWS:

AWS is currently the largest public cloud provider with its server resources named as Elastic Compute Cloud (EC2) and storage resources named as Simple Storage Services (S3). AWS was launched in 2006 and expected to rise to $5 billion business pretty soon. It has data centers across the world in 12 different geographical regions. Amazon's database infrastructure for RDBMS is known as Relational Database Services (RDS).

## Red Hat OpenShift:

OpenShift is a PaaS offering and has 3 different flavors.

a) OpenShift Online – Public PaaS. Has a free plan.
b) OpenShift Origin – Open source platform that forms OpenShift core.

c) OpenShift Enterprise 3 – Private PaaS

OpenShift is built on top of AWS IaaS. It uses Docker and Kubernetes under the hood to deal with containerization and provisioning.

**Microsoft Azure:**

Microsoft Azure provides both PaaS and IaaS. Launched in 2010, Microsoft Azure is also considered as a leader in the IaaS field.

Try Azure for free with $200 in credit.

URL: http://bit.ly/microsoft-azure-1

**IBM Softlayer:**

Soflayer is an IaaS provider and was founded in 2005 and acquired by IBM in 2013. IBM has a PaaS subscription and the service is known as IBM Bluemix.

**Product Engineering:**

Developing and engineering are two different disciplines and I have focused on engineering part in this book. Engineering only gets you a proof of concept where developing gets you the cash churning product. So you would need a complete development process in place after you complete reading this book, to carry on making that cash cow out of your idea that you engineer with the help of this guide/book. Now that we have covered the basics, let us dive into the product aspect and connect the dots as we go further into subsequent chapters. Let us also ask that important question; what does that mean by 'a product' in our context and what exactly is 'product engineering in the cloud'?

A product in our context can be a multi tenant single page application (SPA) built on Java EE platform and offered through web in the form of a Software as a Service. Single page characteristics can be achieved using AngularJS JavaScript framework. Multi tenancy can be achieved using a shared IaaS/PaaS along with an RDS or a No SQL database.

Based on the business model, the application can be enterprise software or consumer software. Generally, if the solution is for indirectly supporting a business, non-profit or education, then it's a non-enterprise application by categorization. Generally termed as a D2C application. Usually the free versions (Freemium business model) of enterprise applications are D2Cs. There is a 3rd category – D2C enterprises. They are generally small and medium sized enterprises (SMEs).

**Product in the Cloud:**

In our context and for our exercise, it is obvious that a 'product in the cloud' means a product running on AWS/OpenShift, ideally a multi tenant SPA and it could have a micro services or a service oriented architecture under the hood.

**Area of focus:**

Some key areas of focus for a cloud based application are the following:

a)  Choice of IaaS/PaaS – This in turn depends on the choice of application stack - a Java stack, .Net stack, a Node JS or a Scala stack. If the application stack is available out of the box and if we intend to have minimal configuration changes, PaaS is the default choice. If we require custom built application stack or if we want more level of control on infrastructure, IaaS seems to be a better choice.

b)  Security – There were a lot of trust issues with cloud based services during the initial stages and even before few years. Cloud industry has grown too big and IT industry in general is educated to a high level on the advantages of moving to cloud even from a security perspective. Access level, data level and infrastructure level security are few extra areas to focus while planning on and on implementing a SaaS based on IaaS/PaaS (which actual means, cloud inside (IaaS/PaaS) and cloud outside (SaaS))

c) Scalability – How quickly an application can be scaled up or scaled down or scaled out is a sure sort question to ask while considering cloud for a product. Scaling at vertical (scale up/down) versus scaling at horizontal (scale out) dimension is what it means to scale.

d) Fail-over and High Availability (HA) – How to add fail over mechanisms and domain configurations in such a way that there is no downtime for a SaaS application through HA.

e) Fault tolerance – How to achieve fault tolerance

f) Availability and SLA – Availability metrics, Response time metrics.

g) Continuous Monitoring – Application performance monitoring (APM), Process-level monitoring, Infrastructure level monitoring and Synthetic (pro-active) monitoring are some areas to consider.

h) Business Continuity Plan (BCP) / Disaster Recovery (DR) - DR Strategy, DR Implementation, DR Testing, DR Exercise.

i) Code-pipeline – Continuous Integration (CI)

and Continuous Delivery (CD), Infrastructure as Code (Docker, Mesosphere, Chef, Ansible, Puppet).

j) Day to day support – Also have a system for toll free phone system such as Ring Central®, Chat system such as Intercom®, Monitoring notifications (alerts) from APM tools such as DynaTrace Ruxit®, New Relic® or Pingdom. Monitoring tools, QA team and Customer support plays a big role in making your product a big success.

**Summary:**

In this introductory chapter, a lot of ground work that needs to be done before planting your idea on to cloud based platform, is covered at breadth. The basics of cloud computing and foundation for engineering a software product on cloud are also covered in this chapter. It is fascinating to learn that categorizing and speaking the cloud terms are easier than the old world infrastructure terminologies. In a nutshell the chapter looks at cloud computing at a perspective from your idea. Some real world organizations are referenced for easy understanding of the big picture. Cloud generally deals with resource provisioning, resource management and networking from infrastructure stand point.

# 2

## PLANTING YOUR IDEA IN THE CLOUD

In the first chapter, we went through the basics of cloud computing, service models deployment models, conventions and some o f the cloud providers presently available in the cloud marketplace. We also took a brief look at product engineering and a quick visualization of the product on cloud infrastructure. Areas to be focused while planning on a product to be hosted in the cloud were also discussed in the first chapter.

Now it's the time to take a step back and bring in our product idea and transform that into a skeleton at first and then a working prototype with the help of this book.

Having a product idea, of course is the very first reason, you started reading this book. As we know knowledge in itself is useless unless directed, organized, and applied. One might have knowledge (knowledge on cloud architecture for example), but that is just the foundation. It needs a direction. Good thing is that having an idea, in the first place itself is a direction. And with that you would know by now where you will end up. You will end up having a real product up-and-running in the cloud. The second thing is organized knowledge. Once you have directed your knowledge, you must organize it into specific plans of action. This chapter deals about that part. i.e., organizing your knowledge about cloud and using that knowledge to form an action. The third thing, applied knowledge, is dealt in further chapters and it will help you in actionizing your organized thoughts and knowledge into a product, engineered in the cloud.

**Turning your idea into technical snapshots:**

Let us take an idea of a multi tenant (tenancy), single page model (delivery model), micro services (architecture), software as a service (offering) that can be hosted on cloud with minimal efforts minimal pricing and with an agile manner.

I am going to consider a crowd sourced ride sharing application that is available only on web for this exercise. In other words a stripped down Uber® ridesharing model for office goers. Ridesharing is the alternative to driving to work alone. It's carpooling, vanpooling, walking, riding your bike or public transit. The most obvious benefit to people who rideshare is the savings in gasoline. This is a consumer model than an enterprise model. Considering this idea of ridesharing, turning it into a web application is a step by step process.

## Pre requisites:

Cloud has become "the new normal" and is transforming how many businesses operate, says AWS Senior Vice President Andy Jassy. In lines with his thoughts, and without having a sales and marketing perspective for AWS, I see an industry in itself in AWS. It is official cloud war time and AWS is winning. To give a quick view into those people in whose head they think what is AWS's server virtualization built on, the answer is Xen hypervisor first developed by University of Cambridge, England.

This chapter is compiled in such a way that we go right from domain search till the end part of going live in production in a nutshell. We don't cover the development part which is more of design and coding / implementation. That's purely up to the Solution Architect (SA) and the Technical Architect (TA) to decide upon. Please remember that this book is specifically target to Enterprise IT Architect (EITA) and Infrastructure Architects (IA).

## Step 1: Domain Search and Setup

There is multiple domain name registrars out there in the market and picking one based on pricing and maintenance is fairly easy. Most of the registrars allow transferring the domain to other domains for free or for a nominal fee. Some of the industry leaders are GoDaddy®, Name.com®, Namecheap.com®, Hover® (Canadian), Gandi® and eNom®.

URLs:
http://bit.ly/domain-registrar-1
http://bit.ly/domain-registrar-2
http://bit.ly/domain-registrar-3
http://bit.ly/domain-registrar-4
http://bit.ly/domain-registrar-5
http://bit.ly/domain-registrar-6

Domain setup is crucial for the success of business.

**Fun fact 1:** Jet.com® (Ecommerce Company) co-founder Marc Lore and Quidsi® co-founder Vinit Bharara were great believers of easily recognizable domain names. Quidsi launched Diaper.com, Wag.com and Soap.com. Quidsi was acquired by Amazon for $540 million in 2010.

**Fun fact 2:** There's a great story behind the domain name tesla.com, and it's likely that Tesla Motors® would pay a fortune for the property. After all, in 2010 Facebook® purchased fb.com for $8.5 million and in 2011 Apple® purchased icloud.com for $4.5 million.

In 2003, when Tesla co-founders Martin Eberhard and Marc Tarpenning (CEO Elon Musk joined the company soon after it was incorporated as an investor) wanted to register the domain (Tesla.com), it was not available and was owned by Stu Grossman, a Nicola Tesla fan. Note: Tesla® gets its name from Nicola Tesla, the Serbian American electrical engineer who invented induction motor.

One of the official blog posts of AWS states that Amazon has entered into a partnership with Tesla Motors to apply one of the key strength of Tesla (battery storage technology) to address power needs in the US West (Northern California) region of AWS data center.

## Step 2: Setting up Infrastructure

At first we talked about getting a domain and now it's time to set up our application's infrastructure in the cloud. Before doing that let us take a quick view of the application that we are discussing about in this book – the crowd sourced ride sharing application. The idea is disruptive in itself. We will look at how to build it on top of AWS infrastructure. We will also see how to build it on a Red Hat OpenShift platform.

## Introduction to the ride sharing reference architecture:

Please note that a Software as a Service (SaaS) reference architecture (RA) is out of scope of this book. In an enterprise ecosystem or in commercial application spectrum, the layers and stacks that are more common is used for the purpose of understanding the application. That will enable us to layer a proper infrastructure.

## Technology Placement:

## User Interface:

Angular JS (Doesn't matter if we use Angular, Node or React JS)

Note: Most of the modern web applications built after 2012 utilizes one of the popular Single Page Application (SPA) frameworks such as Angular or ExtJS, for fluid user experience. And those built years ahead of HTML 5 timeframe and those JSF legacy applications would require an SPA framework for better User Experience (UX). There a multitude of such migrations going on across the industry and the major driving reason for these migrations are the ability of those SPA frameworks to communicate with the web server behind the scenes.

## Services:

Java Micro Services (Matters a bit as a great deal of enterprise and startups run Java for backend services)

Note: The aforementioned SPA frameworks rely on restful web-services to retrieve dynamic data but render the entirety of the application on the browser (client) via JavaScript. Java takes care of the restful web-services part. Netflix and Twitter, for example, mostly use the Java Virtual Machine (JVM) as a platform of micro services. Usually data transport part, or the server response (from Java services) is an XML, JSON or Ajax (HTML). JSON has been adopted as the defacto standard by the industry. Jackson JSON API's takes care of processing JSON data for preparing server response back to the front end JavaScript framework. Micro services are a vast area to discuss. Martin Fowler of ThoughtWorks describes. Sam Newman in his book 'Building Micro services' gives a head start on Micro services. Micro services are small, autonomous services that work together and modeled around business domains.

## APIs:

Apart from API's that are exposed, APIs that are consumed also need to be thought of while designing the system.

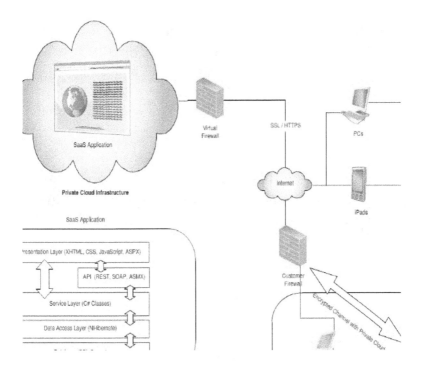

**Figure: 2.1 Topology Diagram**

**Infrastructure:**

Amazon Web Services (AWS). Not just because AWS is pioneer, but AWS provides an easy and agile manner to create account, setup EC2 Instances, security groups and auto scaling. EC2 instances are actually the server VMs of AWS.

## Stack Platform:

Red Hat OpenShift. With the usage of Red Hat OpenShift PaaS, developer is relieved with further operations activity such as application server or web server configurations and setups. OpenShift takes care of getting and setting up the platform itself with a LAMP stack for example (Linux Apache MySQL PHP).

**CI:** Team City®

With cloud-based-applications comes a great continuous integration/deployment/delivery responsibility. JetBrains Team City is used for the exercise.

Jenkins is also a very popular tool that very well fits into this paradigm and practice.

## Containerization:

Docker, the containerization tool is the most talked about tool in recent times. The technology behind containerization is not new. It is almost 10 years or more that this technology has been built and integrated in to Linux in the form of Linux Containers (LXC). Apart from LXCs, which is primarily Linux based similar operating system level virtualization for other UNIX flavored OSes such as Solaris and AIX has also been offered by FreeBSD jails. For AIX it is AIX Workload

Partitions and for Solaris it is Solaris Containers. Nevertheless Docker become synonymous with container technology for the reason that it gradually made itself the most successful and most popular tool for the job.

Docker is an open-source project authored by Solomon Hykes. Docker automates the deployment process for applications using software containers and thus providing an additional layer of abstraction and automation of operating-system-level virtualization on Linux. It uses Linux Kernel's resource isolation features known as CGroups and Kernel Namespaces. File system used is a union-capable file system such as AUF. That allows independent containers to run within a single Linux instance thus avoiding the overhead of starting up, maintaining and shutting down virtual machines.

Essentially, Docker is a tool that packages an application and its dependencies in a virtual container capable of running on any Linux server. This brings in the flexibility and portability features to the product or application on where it can be ran, irrespective of the cloud model i.e., be it on premises, public cloud, private cloud, bare metal or even on a developer laptop.

As the name goes, containers packs everything for the application, and that means, Docker containers wraps up the entire single piece of software in a comprehensive file system with all individual pieces to run it. That means, the code, runtime, system tools, system libraries and dependencies are all packaged into a single logical image named as Docker image. The result is that the application can run on any environment without bothering about the underlying platform or OS or dependencies.

Docker has a lot of similarities with virtualization; however, there is a subtle difference which can be identified from the following diagrams:

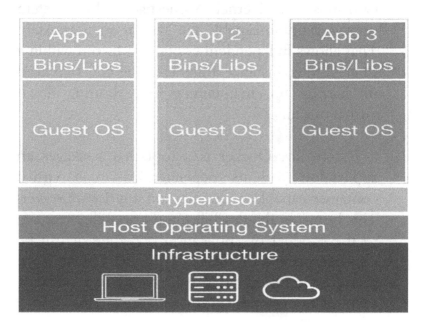

**Figure 2.2 Virtual Machines**

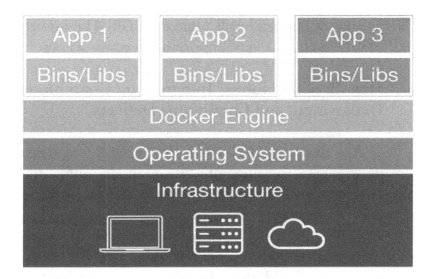

**Figure 2.3 Containers**

In one of their Webinars, Red Hat points that in the next 2 years; more than 90% of technology organizations will make massive investments in technologies such as containerization that directly foster DevOps culture. And when more organizations consider moving to containers, a concrete approach to such kind of workload migration will become as a necessity to ensure successful introduction of a container based cloud platform.

## Infrastructure Management: Chef

Please note that, when you prototype and build your application, reference architecture is important since, like a building built on a weak foundation, an enterprise application built with the wrong architecture will ultimately fail. The choice of architecture is very important, needless to say.

## Step 3: Continuous Integration, Continuous Deployment and Continuous Delivery.

A development practice that mandates developers to integrate their code into the common source code repository several times a day, Continuous Integration (CI), has become synonymous with DevOps practice. In CI, each such source code commit is then verified by an automated build that allows teams to detect any problems early in the product engineering phase.

Continuous Deployment is a practice that is part of the original CI process. Once the application snapshot is built (using Maven/Ant for example) through a CI tool such as Team City (or Jenkins or Hudson or Bamboo), deployments are also taken care of (through a script in most cases), and that is known as Continuous Deployments.

The 3rd piece of this concept is called Continuous Delivery (CD). Continuous delivery (CD) is another software engineering approach that helps teams to produce software products in relatively short product cycles, ensuring that the software product can be reliably released at any time in the cycle. The major focus is on building, testing, and releasing software faster and more frequently. There are multiple tools that provide

CD in a comprehensive package. Thought Works Go is such kind of a CD tool that has got its ground well laid on.

URL: http://bit.ly/cd-tool-1

Setup the tool, setup the necessary job that gets triggered in the CI tool when there is a check-in (code commit). By this step we achieve continuous integration. The whole process comes under DevOps practice. DevOps is a clipped compound of "development" and "operations" in enterprise world.

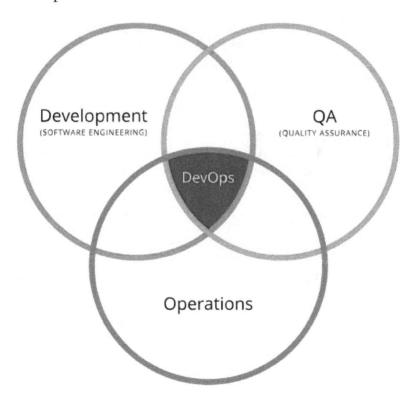

**Figure 2.4 DevOps**

# Step 4: Scaling

Scaling can be achieved in multiple ways. When dealing with AWS, there is an AWS auto scaling feature that can scale out, scale up/down on demand basis.

Scale out is generally termed as horizontal scaling. Involves with adding more servers (EC2 instances or Docker containers).

Scale up is generally termed as vertical scaling. Involves with adding more CPUs or Memory and Hard disk space to the existing infrastructure. Scale down is literally scaling down from horizontal or vertical scaling.

Containerization is a lightweight alternative to full machine virtualization that involves encapsulating an application in a container with its own operating environment. And Docker is the preferred tool and the industry standard at the writing of this book.

By leveraging these steps, the product can be well planted in the cloud and be in the status – up & running.

Summary:

In this chapter, we learned about the steps

involved in taking our product idea from conception to hosting and deploying it in cloud at scale. We also looked at the DevOps practices and containerization concepts / Docker tool to deal with Scaling.

4

# 3

## SETTING UP YOUR APP ON AWS CLOUD

The first chapter and the second have setup the stage for you to build your infrastructure on cloud using a real-world cloud service. This chapter is one of the crucial one that does a walkthrough of setting up the product on Amazon Web Services (AWS). But please note that this book is not an AWS cookbook. This book only helps you in engineering a product right from the conception mode to the deployment mode. This book only helps you get you idea onto cloud in some shape and uses AWS as one vendor from IaaS perspective. You may have to refer to any of those AWS documentation online or AWS books available in marketplace for learning AWS concepts in depth. AWS Reference Architecture Datasheets provide you with the architectural guidance you need in order to build an application that takes full advantage of the AWS cloud infrastructure.

Reference URL: http://bit.ly/aws-architecture-1

## Introduction to AWS:

Most things that used to be hardware are now software! The same is true with computing resources. Environments that were once physical has gone behind the wires and became a logical software platform called the cloud platform.

AWS is a subscription based on-demand pay-as-you-go priced cloud model that allows you to run a server, host a static or dynamic web site or an application, process data, perform data warehousing, handle high volume web traffic and much more. AWS has a broad set of services spread across multiple regions and availability zones.

Each region is a separate geographic area where AWS has a data center. Each region has multiple, isolated locations known as Availability Zones. Placing AWS resources (such as EC2 Instances, Elastic Load Balancers etc) in different regions avoid the single point of failure.

## Major components of AWS:

At the writing of this book, AWS is 10 year old. Last year (in 2015), Gartner, Inc. (an American research and advisory firm providing information technology related insight) estimated that AWS customers are deploying and using 10 times more infrastructure and services on AWS than the combined infrastructure cloud adoption of the next 14 cloud providers. This kind of adoption is never seen in the industry before. And AWS started with minimal services or components in the beginning and exponentially added components as and when there were requests for enhancements.

Before talking about the components, it's important to look back at the history of AWS.

March 14, 2006 was the beginning of a new era in computing. That was the day that Amazon Web Services released the Simple Storage Service (S3). The service was disruptive in the sense that a credit card was all that was needed to sign up and start working on AWS cloud. There was no required proposal for financial approval, there was no RFP, no vendor selection process, no vendor negotiation, and no data center space need be found. And thus S3 became the first official cloud component of AWS!

Storage was first but compute was to follow shortly. And the compute piece is called EC2 (Elastic Compute Cloud). It is one of the key components of AWS and was developed by a small team in a satellite development office in South Africa. Developed first for Amazon's internal infrastructure, it currently stands out as one of the building block and standing pillar for AWS.

Ironically, EC2 started out as an idea of Chris Pinkham, who worked as an engineer in charge of Amazon's global infrastructure in the early 2000s. Chris later left Amazon and co-founded Nimbula, a provider of private cloud infrastructure management software. Nimbula was later acquired by Oracle (in 2013).

Please note that AWS was evolved out of a paper presentation by Chris Pinkham and Benjamin Black in late 2003. AWS EC2 was built by Pinkham's team and by lead developer Chris Brown in Cape Town, South Africa.

Following are the products and services that form the components of AWS:

- Computing components
- Storage & Content Delivery

- Database

- Networking

- Developer Tools

- Management Tools

- Security & Identity

- Analytics

- Internet of Things

- Game Development

- Mobile Services

- Application Services

- Enterprise Applications

We will quickly go through each of these components to get a birds view of the large landscape of AWS.

**Computing components:**

There are majorly 4 computing components in AWS.

Compute

EC2
Virtual Servers in the Cloud

EC2 Container Service
Run and Manage Docker Containers

Elastic Beanstalk
Run and Manage Web Apps

Lambda
Run Code in Response to Events

**Figure 3.1 AWS Computing Components**

i) Elastic Compute Cloud (EC2)

Scalable on demand virtual private servers. AWS engineers implemented EC2 using Xen virtualization method. Classification of EC2 instances:

a) Spot Instances

Spot instances are a type of EC2 instance that enables bidding process on unused EC2 instances. This helps in lowering Amazon EC2 costs at a significant manner. Amazon sets the hourly price for a Spot instance (of each instance type in each Availability Zone). However the pricing fluctuates depending on the supply of Spot instances and the demand for Spot instances at real time. In effect, your spot instance gets spinned up whenever your bid exceeds the current market price.

b) Reserved Instances

Amazon EC2 Reserved Instances allow you to reserve Amazon EC2 computing capacity for 1 or 3 years, in return for a discounted price of up to 75% of the price compared to On-Demand instances.

Reserved Instances can significantly lower your computing costs for your workloads and provide a capacity reservation so that you can have confidence in your ability to launch the number of instances you have reserved when the demand hits.

c) Scheduled Instances

Scheduled (and reserved) instances are a new type of offering in AWS that allow you to reserve capacity on a recurring basis with a daily, weekly, or monthly schedule over the course of a one-year term. After you complete your purchase, the instances are available to launch during the time windows that you specified.

d) Dedicated Hosts

It's a kind of bare metal physical server with EC2 capability. In other words an Amazon EC2 Dedicated Host stands out as a physical server with EC2 capacities and is just as the named indicates – dedicated host. Dedicated Hosts can help you address compliance requirements and reduce costs by allowing you to use your existing server-bound software licenses.

e) Commands

Commands are a computing utility available in AWS to remotely administer your EC2 instances.

ii) EC2 Container Service (ECS)

Amazon ECS is of course a service made to run Docker containers on cluster mode. ECS makes it easy to deploy, manage, and scale Docker containers running applications, services, and batch processes. Amazon ECS places containers across your cluster based on your resource needs and is integrated with familiar features like Elastic Load Balancing, EC2 security groups, EBS volumes and IAM roles.

iii) Elastic Beanstalk

Elastic Beanstalk is a Platform as a Service offering from Amazon Web Services that allows users to create applications and push them to a definable set of AWS services. It's an equivalent for Red Hat OpenShift. At the time of writing this book. Following platforms are available on Beanstalk.

Preconfigured
  Java
  Node.js
  PHP
  Python
  Ruby
  Tomcat
  IIS
  Go
Preconfigured – Docker
  GlassFish
  Go
  Python
Generic
  Docker
  Multi-container Docker

**Figure 3.2 Beanstalk available platforms**

iv) Lambda

AWS Lambda is a new computing service from Amazon that runs developer's scripts in response to events and it automatically manages the compute resources for them. This process of auto management makes it easy to build applications that respond quickly to event based scripts/code.

## Storage & Content Delivery:

There are majorly 6 storage and content delivery components in AWS.

Storage & Content Delivery

**S3**
Scalable Storage in the Cloud

**CloudFront**
Global Content Delivery Network

**Elastic File System** PREVIEW
Fully Managed File System for EC2

**Glacier**
Archive Storage in the Cloud

**Import/Export Snowball**
Large Scale Data Transport

**Storage Gateway**
Hybrid Storage Integration

**Figure 3.3 AWS Storage & Content Delivery Components**

i)   Simple Storage Service (S3)

S3 is an online file storage web service offered by AWS.

It's easy for a new comer to cloud space to get confused between S3 and other online storage subscriptions such as Dropbox®, Google Drive®, Apple iCloud® and Microsoft OneDrive®. They are entirely 2 different types of storage services. S3 is designed for heavy weight server environments and not for most home users, whereas Dropbox, Google Drive and its kind are designed for home users or for business users depending on the subscription you choose.

Therefore S3 is actually not your consumer-friendly cloud storage. It's a storage service (object storage) designed to be accessed programmatically. You have to build something on top of it to really make it usable by a human. In fact some of the other consumer-friendly cloud storage applications are built on top of S3.

Netflix uses S3 to store their streaming movies. They're served from a CDN, but the base copies are in S3.

**Fun fact:** Dropbox as well uses S3 and I was really amazed at the pricing strategy of Dropbox. Dropbox pro sells at $9.99 a month for 1TB of storage, whereas S3, the underlying storage service is sold at $30 for standard storage option. Devil in the details will tell you the reason behind it is that none of the customers use up to 1TB and hence Dropbox does not have to pay $30 for 1 TB per month. On top of it, the pricing can be negotiated with AWS for large environments such as in the case of Dropbox. While placing your product in the right pricing strategy is not in the scope of this book, it is a very important aspect to consider while the product goes live and is ready for user on boarding.

ii)   CloudFront

Amazon has gotten on to almost all money making areas of cloud. CDN services is another key major money making cloud services that Amazon has factored in to support high traffic marketing websites and consumer applications. CloudFront is a global content delivery network (CDN) service from AWS that integrates well with other Amazon Web Service's services and products. Cloud Front facilitates low latency, high data transfer speeds, and no minimum usage commitments for its customers and thus making it a top choice for many major websites that currently uses Fastly, Akamai, MaxCDN etc. Note: All of these providers are considered as world's largest CDN providers. One useful use case for CloudFront is to distribute content while building a Content Management System (CMS) such as Wordpress® or Drupal®.

iii) Elastic File System

Amazon Elastic File System (Amazon EFS) is a service storing files for Amazon Elastic Compute Cloud (Amazon EC2) instances. Amazon EFS is easy to use and provides a simple interface that allows you to create and configure file systems quickly and easily.

At the writing of this book, this feature is only available in Preview and is supported only in US West (Oregon) region.

iv) Glacier

Amazon Glacier is a secure, durable, and extremely low-cost cloud storage service for data archiving and long-term backup.

v) Snowball

Snowball is a rugged physical storage appliance introduced by AWS for importing data to AWS. The appliance is a bit larger than an old-school desktop case and it can hold up to 50 terabytes of data. It has a Kindle on the side, which functions as an automatic shipping label. Amazon says the case can withstand a 6 G jolt and is entirely self-contained, with a 110-volt power supply and 10 GB network connection built-in. AWS using Amazon-provided secure appliances for transport.

Snowball is an elegant solution to large scale data migrations from existing data center to AWS. Shipping partner is UPS.

**Figure 3.4 AWS Snowball**

vi) Storage Gateway

The AWS Storage Gateway is an on-premises virtual appliance that provides seamless and secure integration between your on-premises applications and AWS's storage infrastructure. The service enables you to securely upload data to the AWS cloud for scalable and cost-effective storage.

## Database:

There are currently 5 database components in AWS.

Database

**RDS**
Managed Relational Database Service

**DynamoDB**
Managed NoSQL Database

**ElastiCache**
In-Memory Cache

**Redshift**
Fast, Simple, Cost-Effective Data Warehousing

**DMS**
Managed Database Migration Service

**Figure 3.4 AWS Database**

i)   RDS

Amazon Relational Database Service (Amazon RDS) is a web service that makes it easier to set up, operate, and scale a relational database in the cloud. It provides cost-efficient, resizable capacity for an industry-standard relational database and manages common database administration tasks. Supported databases are:

a) Amazon Aurora

b) MySQL Community Edition

c) MariaDB Community Edition

d) PostgreSQL

e) Oracle

    i.   Oracle Enterprise Edition

    ii.   Oracle Standard Edition

    iii.   Oracle Standard Edition One

    iv.   Oracle Standard Edition Two

f) Microsoft SQL Server

    a. MS SQL Server Express Edition

    b. MS SQL Server Web Edition

    c. MS SQL Server Standard Edition

    d. MS SQL Server Enterprise Edition

ii) DynamoDB

Amazon DynamoDB is a fast and flexible NoSQL database service for all applications that need consistent, single-digit millisecond latency at any scale. Its flexible data model and reliable performance make it a great fit for mobile, web, gaming, ad-tech, Internet of Things (IoT) and many other applications.

## iii) ElastiCache

Elastic cache service from AWS that runs on cluster mode. Supported DBEngines: Memcached and Redis.

## iv) Redshift

Amazon Redshift is a fast, fully managed, petabyte-scale data warehouse solution that makes it simple and cost-effective to efficiently analyze all your data using your existing business intelligence tools.

## v) DMS

Amazon DynamoDB is a fast and flexible NoSQL database service for all applications that need consistent, single-digit millisecond latency at any scale. Its flexible data model and reliable performance make it a great fit for mobile, web, gaming, ad-tech, IoT, and many other applications.

AWS Chief Evangelist Jeff Barr who writes AWS blog and did a AWS Road Trip in 2013, says that DMS is for those who would like to move their existing on-premises data centre infrastructure to the AWS cloud with virtually no downtime.

## Networking:

There are currently 3 networking components in AWS.

**Figure 3.5 AWS Networking Components**

i)    VPC

Amazon Virtual Private Cloud (Amazon VPC) lets you set up a private cloud (a private, isolated section) within the Amazon Web Services (AWS) cloud computing service. Using Amazon VPC, organizations can launch AWS resources in a virtual network topology.

ii)   Direct Connect

AWS Direct Connect is a network service using which data that would have previously been transported over the Internet can now is delivered through a private network connection between AWS and your datacenter or corporate network.

iii)  Route 53

Route 53 is Amazon's Domain Name System (DNS). One of the key features of Route 53 is programmatic access to the service that allows customers to modify DNS records via web service calls. We can setup rules in such a way that if a region in which our instances are located is blacked out; we can automatically switch traffic to a secondary (Disaster Recovery) environment to carry on with Business Continuity Plan (BCP).

We have covered computing, storage, database and networking services of AWS. The other components such as the Developer Tools, Management Tools, Security & Identity, Analytics, IoT, Game Development, Mobile Services,

Application Services and Enterprise Applications are not to be covered here due to the reason that this book is not essentially an AWS reference book, but a guide to help you setup your product idea on cloud using AWS and using Red Hat OpenShift. There are numerous AWS books and materials available in market place to get a first hand hold on AWS in depth.

**Figure 3.6 AWS Management Console**

## Aspects of interest:

What aspects of AWS are we interested in is an interesting question to ask ourselves. Answer to it is that it depends on use case by use case on what component to choose for delivering the product on cloud. But there are some core concepts that you would anyhow use are covered in the previous section.

Following are of importance and of interest to us to walk the example of ride sharing application on cloud.

EC2 instances vs. Elastic Beanstalk. That's the first step to decide on. If we are planning to get server (VM) resources and manage it, EC2 is the way to go. EC2 gives more control as well. If the priority is fast deployments without bothering on the internals, Elastic Beanstalk is the way to go. Again, you will have to check if your platform is supported in Beanstalk.

In this book we take EC2 instances for setting up our production environment on AWS.

IAM (Identity & Access Management) is another important piece that needs to be taken care of while dealing with AWS cloud.

IAM takes care of API Key security, Identity Management, Key Management, Policy to be applied for authorizations etc.

Using RDS as a database instance is a power to the game. If NoSQL is in the plans, use DynamoDB or use MongoDB installed on an EC2 instance (MongoDB setup preferably in replica set model).

S3 will also take main stage for product engineering in the cloud.

Now that we know the major components of AWS and those components that we are interested in, it's time to roll up the sleeves and try some hands-on exercises on AWS.

**Step by step process for setting up server infrastructure:**

Infrastructure is all about supporting workload requirements of applications.

Let us walk step by step through infrastructure setup on AWS.

**AWS account creation:**

First and foremost, navigate to AWS landing page and create an account. URL: http://bit.ly/aws-setup-1

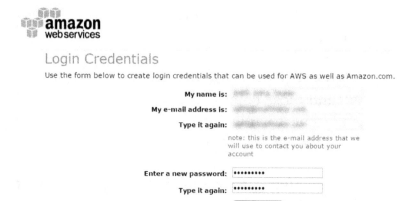

**Figure 3.7 AWS Sign Up Screen**

Sign up process will take you through the following steps as in the screenshot.

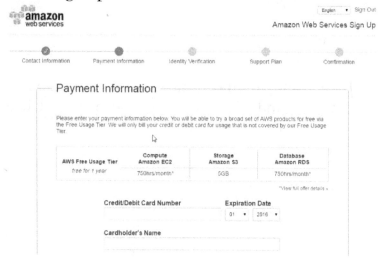

**Figure 3.8 AWS Sign Up Process**

Please note that AWS require a credit card to signup, of course. AWS is free for a year if you run minimal resources of every component. Number of hours equals about 730 hours every month. AWS provides 750 hours per month of Linux, RHEL, or SLES t2.micro instance usage for free on EC2. And similarly, 5GB of standard storage S3, 750 hours of RDS and so on. That implies you can run a minimum viable product in AWS for free for a year. With more number of instances and resources, of course AWS bill goes up and it's very much variable based on your usage.

## Billing:

On AWS, Billing and Cost Management is done using the AWS Billing and Cost Management service. It facilitates AWS customer in paying the AWS bills. It also helps in monitoring the usage and also helps in budgeting/estimating the costs.

A credit card needs to be put on file and then the billing service automatically charges the credit card on file. There are multiple card types available for billing. It's invoiced on a monthly basis and hence the charges appear on your credit card bill monthly. The credit card information can be viewed or updated at any time and it is also possible to designate a different credit card for AWS to charge on the Payment Methods page in the Billing and Cost Management AWS console.

It is notable to mention that every AWS account gets free tier for the first year.

## Note:

And if you sign up for a new account and choose India for your contact address, your user agreement will be with Amazon Internet Services Pvt. Ltd (AISPL), a local AWS seller in India. AISPL will manage your billing, and your invoice total will be listed in rupees instead of dollars. Note that after you create an account with AISPL, you can't change the country in your contact information.

## Support:

There are 3 support models from AWS.

i)  Developer Support
    Support for experimental use.
    Pricing: $49 per month.
ii) Business Support
    Support for production use.
    Pricing: $100 per month base price and upwards depending on usage.
iii) Enterprise Support
    Support for business critical use.
    Pricing: $15000 per month base price and upwards depending on usage.

## Multiple accounts:

There are various use cases for having multiple AWS accounts.

Use case #1: Your organization has multiple products and you want to segregate each product into a separate AWS account. This helps in managing each product individually.

Use case #2: Each product has multiple environments and you want development environment in one AWS account and production environment in another AWS account.

Use case #3: Geography based segregation for AWS accounts depending on business requirements.

For all of the above uses cases and for more, you may choose to have multiple accounts and use consolidated billing if you would like to receive a single invoice for all your accounts.

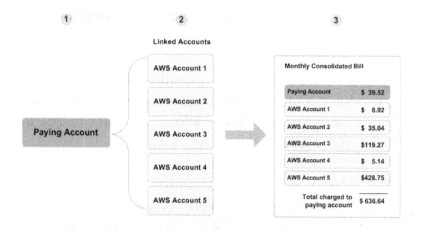

**Figure 3.9 AWS Consolidated Billing**

For example, Netflix uses multiple accounts which allow them to create a hard separation between deployment environments. It also allows them to negotiate different guarantees from Amazon for different purposes.

**Fun fact 1:** Netflix uses a custom console and not AWS console to manage cloud resources. And Netflix, of course, has multiple AWS accounts. It's named as Asgard. Asgard is a web interface for application deployments and cloud management in Amazon Web Services (AWS). It is essentially a PaaS and something like OpenShift.

URL: http://bit.ly/netflix-asgard-github

**Fun fact 2:** Adrian Cockcroft was the cloud architect at Netflix and a leading proponent of AWS. He is the one who engineered and developed Netflix into a full blown Cloud organization. Netflix is also a total OSS (Open Source Software) and a DevOps oriented organization. Cockcroft has often given talks on 'planning ahead of a disaster' and developed 'Chaos Monkey Architecture' at Netflix to randomly kill instances or zones to test resilience. It's called 'Simian Army'. Netflix is one among the top 10 premium customers of AWS. Netflix generates roughly one third of North American web traffic and peaks at Sunday Night. In early January 2016, Netflix shutdown it's last data center and hence marked closure of cloud migration that spanned 7 years.

URL: http://bit.ly/netflix-cloud-migration

In many respects, Netflix has benchmark architecture for running a large enterprise on AWS.

### Choosing AWS Regions:

How to choose regions for your instances or for your environment is an important question to consider.

Physical location of cloud players is increasingly important for global enterprises, as many countries have laws that forbid data from being stored in other countries.

You may choose the closest available for customer where data privacy rules come into play. And you may choose the closest available region for that customer for a production environment. You may similarly choose the closest region for developers for development environment and so on.

With 13 different geographical regions and 35 availability zones and still more getting added year by year, AWS has one of the largest distributed data center network. Out of the currently available 12 geographical regions, the US regions are US East (Northern Virginia), where the majority of AWS servers are based, US West (northern California) and US West (Oregon). Other regions are Brazil (São Paulo), Europe (Ireland and Germany), Southeast Asia (Singapore), East Asia (Tokyo, Seoul, Beijing), Asia (Mumbai, India) and Australia (Sydney). Apart from the above, there is a government variant named "Gov Cloud", based in the Northwestern United States, provided for U.S. government customers, complementing existing government agencies already using the US East Region. AWS has announced another 5 Regions (and 11 Availability Zones) in Canada, China, India, Ohio, and the United Kingdom coming online throughout the next year. Each Region is wholly contained within a single country and all of its data and services stay within the designated Region.

**Figure 3.1: AWS Global Infrastructure**

## Traffic patterns:

If you use Elastic Load Balancer (ELB) in AWS, you can use its access logs to understand traffic patterns to ELB and underlying Apache/Nginx/IIS server. With data from access logs that has traffic patterns; AWS region that is optimal for the application can also be decided.

## Geographies:

AWS offers regional endpoints to reduce data latency in applications and the choice of endpoints should be based on this factor. Amazon Web Services' regional endpoint is a URL that is the entry point for a web service. Take for example; https://dynamodb.us-west-2.amazonaws.com is an entry point for the DynamoDB service in AWS.

Some other services, such as IAM, however do not support region. Their endpoints do not include a region and is often considered as part of the Global Region. Some services, such as Amazon EC2, also let you specify an endpoint that does not include a specific region. That will default it to AWS's oldest and first region – North Virginia which is categorized as US East -1. For example, https://ec2.amazonaws.com is routed to us-east-1.

Unlike virtually every other technology infrastructure provider, each AWS Region has multiple Availability Zones and data centers. In addition to replicating applications and data across multiple data centers in the same Region using Availability Zones, you can also choose to increase redundancy and fault tolerance further by replicating data between geographic Regions. Throughout the next year, the AWS Global Infrastructure will expand with at least 11 new Availability Zones in new geographic Regions: India, Montreal in Canada, Ningxia in China, Ohio in North America, and the United Kingdom.

## CDN usage:

Amazon CloudFront is a global content delivery network (CDN) service. It integrates with other Amazon Web Services products to give developers and businesses an easy way to distribute content to end users with low latency, high data transfer speeds, and no minimum usage commitments.

AWS WAF is a web application firewall that helps protect your web applications from common web exploits that could affect application availability, compromise security, or consume excessive resources. AWS WAF gives you control over which traffic to allow or block to your web applications by defining customizable web security rules.

### CMS example - Word press:

An example for the real use of CDN is while setting up a blog site or a marketing site, for example, using Wordpress. Wordpress is a free and open-source content management system (CMS) based on PHP and MySQL. It is one of the world's largest and popular blogging systems in CMS ecosystem.

### How to set up EC2 instances?

Setting up EC2 instances are as simple as launching a selected server profile (RHEL/Windows/Ubuntu/Custom AMI) from AWS management console. AWS documentation has step by step process to help with this. Following are the 5 steps prior to setting up EC2 instances:

i.   Sign Up for AWS

ii.   Create an IAM User - Optional
iii.  Create a Key Pair
iv.   Create a Virtual Private Cloud (VPC) -
      Optional
v.    Create a Security Group

It is out of the scope for this book to cover detailed steps in setting up an EC2 instance. This book is intended as a guide for you to get an idea on what to do or help you decide on infrastructure setups and supported technology stack side on cloud. This chapter specifically deals that from AWS perspective.

## How to setup security groups?

A security group acts as a virtual firewall to control the traffic for its associated instances. To use a security group, you add the inbound rules to control incoming traffic to the instance, and outbound rules to control the outgoing traffic from your instance. To associate a security group with an instance, you specify the security group when you launch the instance. If you add and remove rules from the security group, we apply those changes to the instances associated with the security group automatically.

Please note that security groups inbound outbound rules setup to be configured with utmost caution. If port 22 is wide open, there is a greater chance for brute force attacks and if an intruder service gets access to the EC2 instance, it can initiate pings to other EC2 instances in the network and that may arise in an abuse ticket from AWS. AWS can shutdown the instance or block access to the account if this is not properly taken care of when an abuse is reported.

## How does AMI help in disaster recovery, backups and restore etc?

AMI stands for Amazon Machine Image. AMI provides the information required to launch an EC2 instance. You specify an AMI when you launch an instance, and you can launch as many instances from the AMI as you need. You can also launch instances from as many different AMIs as you need.

For example, you launched an RHEL AMI EC2 instance. And you want to take a backup of that image. You may create an AMI from the running instance and it creates an AMI (a custom AMI) from your RHEL AMI instance and that can be used to launch copies of your first and original RHEL instance. This is a killer feature that helps in disaster recovery; AMI backup and AMI restore process.

It is a best practice to periodically create AMI from existing running EC2 instances and copy it over to other regions. That will help in achieving disaster recovery in case of an outage in the primary region. You can very well use the AMIs copied to the other (secondary) region and point your DNS to the new image, for example.

**Backups**

Periodically take snapshots of AMI for backups of images.

**Load balancers (AWS Elastic Load Balancer – ELB):**

Amazon provides load balancers in clustered mode that can scale up or scale down based on traffic and hence named as elastic load balancer. Please ensure that you create Listeners for port 80/443 in ELB to route your ELB traffic to a web server running on an EC2 instance. Without listeners on listening mode, ELB will not function as expected.

**Domain:**

Amazon's domain registrar service is called Route 53. Apart from domain registrations, it also helps in creating rules for architecting disaster recovery. For example, create a rule that states that when the service is down on a primary server, route it to a secondary server in a different region.

It is not mandatory to use this feature. You may have your domain created in GoDaddy, for example and use Route 53 for DR setup.

## DR:

Disaster recovery (DR) involves a set of policies and procedures to enable the recovery or continuation of vital technology infrastructure and systems following a natural or human-induced disaster.

Disaster Recovery as a Service (DRaaS) is an emerging business model with high cloud adaption by smaller startups to larger Fortune 500 organizations. DRaaS is nothing but Disaster Recovery running on cloud. Using DRaaS also means the organization doesn't have to invest in -- and maintain -- their own off-site DR environment as in our previous examples, listed in above sections.

The AWS cloud supports many popular disaster recovery (DR) architectures.

More details can be read on the following URL: http://bit.ly/aws-dr-1

## Auto scaling:

Auto Scaling is built into AWS. Auto Scaling facilitates to maintain application availability at desired SLAs and allows scaling your Amazon EC2 capacity higher or lower in automatic manner according to the conditions defined in configurations. Auto Scaling can be used to help ensure that you are running your desired number of Amazon EC2 instances at any given point of time. Whenever there is a demand spike Auto Scaling can also automatically activate itself and increase the number of Amazon EC2 instances to maintain performance. Similarly it can be run to decrease capacity during non business hours or non peak hours to reduce costs. Auto Scaling is well suited both to applications that have stable demand patterns or that experience hourly, daily, or weekly variability in usage.

Note: Be careful while configuring AWS auto scaling groups since with unintelligent use of threshold values, AWS may create too many EC2 instances and scale up rapidly and result in high number of hours or vice versa (too less EC2 instances with improper scaling and performance issues as a by-product).

## Configuring SSL:

With your idea as a product on cloud, SSL is a very crucial step to get authenticity on your product and also to get product certifications, if you plan so or even payment gateway integrations. Non SSL URL's are generally not trusted (a well known fact). You may purchase SSL from Certificate Authority (CA) or from resellers. Some examples of resellers who sell SSL for subsidized prices are the following:

URL: http://bit.ly/ssls-1
URL: http://bit.ly/domain-registrar-3

It is very common that Domain Registrars usually resell SSLs. In some cases, for example, GoDaddy has their own SSLs. Popular SSL CA companies are Symantec, Geotrust, and Comodo etc.

Also getting the right SSL also make sense. An extended validation (EV) SSL will get you green bar with the company name on Chrome or Firefox browser for example. This gives the visitor (end-user) of your product a high security assurance. There are multiple other factors to consider while planning on SSL such as going for a wildcard SSL or a SAN SSL. These topics can be researched online and is out of scope for this book.

**Caution:**

A quick setup can be easily done on AWS. But caution needs to be exercised in architecting failover, resiliency, high availability, disaster recovery etc. Proper use of Load balancers, Auto Scaling, Docker containers, AMI backups, Cross Region setup etc avoids such catastrophic issues.

Another question to ask you is how to avoid cloud provider/vendor lock-in. A cross usage of cloud provider, for example, using AWS as a base/primary environment, and using OpenShift as a secondary disaster recovery environment will also help in addressing both availability concerns and vendor lock-in concerns.

However, Netflix for example, used only AWS and thereby they created informal RFPs for AWS and thereby driving AWS to provide many killer features as we have today. An interesting article on how Netflix fixed AWS when AWS was not capable enough for Netflix requirements, rather than moving to OpenStack. However please note that content delivery (the most critical part of Netflix) runs on Netflix OpenConnect (customized open source CDN of Netflix).

URL: http://bit.ly/netflix-usecase-1

**Fun Facts:**

Did you know that there are 6 cities named after cloud in the United States of America? Most of these cities are actually named after a Roman Catholic saint from France, Saint Cloud, also known as Clodoald. He was the son of the Frankish king Chlodomer.

1.  St. Cloud, Minnesota

2. St. Cloud, Florida
3. St. Cloud, Missouri
4. St. Cloud, Wisconsin and
5. Saint Cloud, West Virginia

And when you are in New York City, nothing beats being at the upscale bar on The Knickerbocker Hotel rooftop at Times Square, named after late 19th century hotel that originally occupied the site.

**Summary:**

In this chapter, AWS is covered in breadth starting from introduction to real time use cases and components to their applications in real world enterprises.

A lot of features of AWS and the most important areas to focus on infrastructure for product engineering in the cloud are covered in this chapter. And hence this chapter enables the reader to use reference architecture (RA) of AWS or use custom reference architecture to setup the product on AWS.

With a strong base on AWS and a prototype setup on AWS after reading this chapter, the reader can read further chapters that talks about functional and non functional use cases from infrastructure perspective, Application Performance Monitoring (APM) for availability and response time metrics, setting up a real Disaster Recovery (DR) architecture, DevOps principles such as CI/CD, Using OpenShift Platform (PaaS) as an alternative to AWS, production support aspects for the product and much more.

# 4

## APPLICATION PERFORMANCE
## MONITORING IN THE CLOUD


Application performance management (APM) is the monitoring and management of performance and availability of software applications. APM is a must-need for sophisticated and scalable applications.

APM strives to detect and diagnose complex application performance problems to maintain an expected level of service. Application performance monitoring and management software helps organizations and businesses collect and monitor data on all fronts of an application's performance. Thus APM is "the translation of IT metrics into business aspects".

In this chapter we will cover the theory behind

APM and some real world monitoring tools in the enterprise ecosystem. The competitive landscape of APM is over crowded with a lot of tools. Some of the top companies in this space are:

i) DynaTrace
ii) Compuware Gomez
iii) DynaTrace Ruxit
iv) New Relic
v) Pingdom
vi) App Dynamics
vii) Data Dog
viii) Fog Light
ix) River Bed
x) App Neta
xi) Logic Monitor
xii) Catchpoint
xiii) Icinga
xiv) Nagios
xv) Copper Egg

And many more.

Measuring application performance comes in 2 flavors:

i) Measuring Performance Metrics on User Experience
ii) Measuring Performance Metrics on Computing Resource

The former usually deals with response time and

average page load time. The later usually deals with infrastructure level metrics such as CPU utilization, Memory consumption and Process monitoring.

APM is one of the key areas to focus on while engineering and developing a web scale product that will run from the cloud. And interestingly most of the tools I mentioned above come with AWS integration through AWS IAM APIs.

In their APM Conceptual Framework, Gartner Research describes five dimensions of APM:

i) End user experience monitoring – (active and passive)
ii) Application runtime architecture discovery and modeling
iii) User-defined transaction profiling (also called business transaction management)
iv) Application component monitoring
v) Reporting & Application data analytics

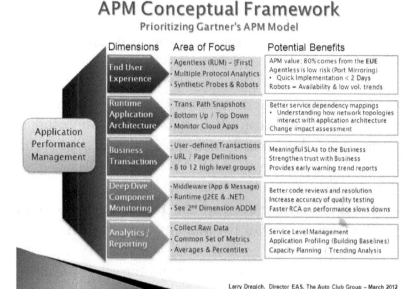

**Figure 4.1: Gartner APM Conceptual Framework**

The APM space has come a long way from a handful of tools such as packet sniffer and tcpdump in the late 1980s to a full blown industry with DynaTrace, New Relic and Riverbed in the current generation – the cloud generation.

APM industry makes sure that the Cloud industry gets going without hiccups. It does so by building sustainable APM solutions and anchoring it into the IT culture, in both enterprise and the start-ups culture.

**Active versus Passive Monitoring:**

Active monitoring is nothing but simulated monitoring. Web transactions, web URL navigations, web application access etc are simulated and monitored. This type of monitoring gives first hand data on the uptime, availability and at times the response time of the web transactions or bare minimum web URLs. Active monitoring is also known as Synthetic Monitoring.

Passive monitoring is nothing but real user monitoring rather than simulated. This can be performed using JavaScript injection into the web pages that needs to be monitored and when a real user access these pages, the monitoring tool records and populates data on to monitoring dashboard with actual user experience. The data might consists of page load times from user's location, user's browser, device, network, and many more such metrics for knowing the performance of that page from actual user's device.

## Service Level Agreement (SLA) and Key Performance Indicator (KPI):

SLA is often an agreement between 2 parties such as the company committing 99.9% uptime and availability of a SaaS product, for instance, to its customers. And KPI is something that the company uses for internal purpose to measure its success such as 100% end to end infrastructure monitoring for being proactive in achieving 99.99% uptime SLA. Monitoring helps in alerting operations team in case of a problem and thence mitigating availability.

SLA is a delivery measurement and KPI is a performance measurement, in other terms. SLA's drives KPI's.

While considering a product infrastructure on cloud, that is more prone to outages than a traditional data center, monitoring and SLA/KPI derivations are much more important than in a conventional product running on premises.

**AWS Marketplace:**

AWS Marketplace is an online store that directly sells third party software prepackaged on AWS cloud. It helps customers find, buy, and immediately start using the software and services that run in the EC2 cloud. One example is a Data Dog Ops Monitoring tool available in AWS on our choice of EC2 type – small/medium/large instances.

URL: http://bit.ly/aws-marketplace-datadog

A ZDNet articles states that AWS Marketplace is kind of Amazon's Juggernaut and since its launch Amazon has started breaking out AWS financials. Marketplace is indeed very helpful to get tools quick started without much groundwork from infrastructure area.

## Summary:

In this chapter, pretty much short and sweet, we took insights into APM space and walked through the basic concepts that makes up APM industry. We also looked at the names of some of the real world APM tools used for monitoring web applications. And then an overview on the important aspects of APM conceptual framework was iterated quickly in this chapter. Key differences between active and passive monitoring were also covered for the better understanding of synthetic versus real user monitoring. Another area that we quickly looked into is SLA versus KPI. All of these make sense for managing the infrastructure for the product hosted in the cloud.

# 5

## SCALING PRINCIPLES AND DISASTER RECOVERY ARCHITECTURE ON AWS CLOUD

In the landscape of cloud based product engineering, one of the most necessary and sought-after feature is the ability to scale. There are surely different ways to accomplish scaling, which is a transformation that increases capabilities or diminishes capabilities. Increasing is for supporting the traffic or hit rates. Diminishing is for cost effectiveness. Among the different ways to get scaling in practice, one is vertical scaling and the other is horizontal scaling. We will go in detail on both of these features in the later part of this chapter.

Scalability in general is the capability of a system, network, or process to handle a growing amount of work, or its potential to be enlarged in order to accommodate that growth.

In philosophy, scaling up often changes the nature of what you are doing. Hence my 2 cents is that you evaluate whether the scaled-up version works as well as the original version. Scaling a business can be thrilling and exhilarating – but it also can be exhausting. This also applies to IT as well. However the same philosophy does not necessarily relate to cloud. In cloud terms, it only gets complex for orchestration and governance. And there could be weak points which makes it necessary to run a vulnerability tests (security aspects) to ensure scaled up cloud business is running good, really good.

In cloud computing, scaling is synonymous to elasticity. Elasticity is defined as "the degree to which a system is able to adapt to workload changes by provisioning and de-provisioning resources in an autonomic manner, such that at each point in time the available resources match the current demand as closely as possible".

Another term associated with scaling is Hyperscale. Hyperscale is the ability of architecture to scale appropriately as increased demand is added to the system. This typically involves the ability to seamlessly provision and add compute, memory, networking, and storage resources to a given node or set of nodes that make up a larger computing, distributed computing, or grid computing environment. Hyperscale computing is necessary in order to build a robust and scalable cloud, big data, map reduce, or distributed storage system and is often associated with the infrastructure required to run large distributed sites such as Facebook, Google, Microsoft or Amazon.

Multi-tenant systems definitely need scaling features. This is because, in most multi-tenant reference architectures, resources are needed only when a new tenant signs up.

**Note:** Wikipedia description on multi-tenancy: The term "software multitenancy" refers to a software architecture in which a single instance of software runs on a server and serves multiple tenants.

Most of the cloud platforms are elastic and AWS has the nomenclature added to most of the products they have such as Elastic Compute Cloud, Elastic Load Balancer etc.

The term auto-scaling was introduced, and the concept popularized, by Amazon Web Services, which offers auto scaling to its users. Auto scaling on Amazon Web Services is done through their command line tool.

In April 2008, Amazon open-sourced Scalr, its

framework for load balancing and auto scaling.

On-demand video provider Netflix has documented their successful use of auto scaling with Amazon Web Services to meet their highly variable consumer needs. They found that aggressive scaling up and delayed and cautious scaling down served their goals of uptime and responsiveness best. For parts of their infrastructure and specific workloads, they found that use of predictive analytics gave even better results. Their software, Scryer, is not available to the public. A Swedish company called Elastisys offers such a predictive auto scaling service, which is compatible with Amazon Web Services and OpenStack.

In an article for TechCrunch, Zev Laderman, the co-founder and CEO of Newvem, a service that helps optimize AWS cloud infrastructure, recommended that startups use auto scaling in order to keep their Amazon Web Services costs low.

A Dutch company named Treestle provides auto scaling on AWS, Rackspace, Interroute VDC and Apache CloudStack. Treestle auto scaling is based on page load time, as opposed to traditional auto scaling solutions that scale based on server statistics policies.

URL: http://bit.ly/treestle

## Vertical versus Horizontal Scaling:

Horizontal scaling means that you scale by adding more machines into your pool of resources where vertical scaling means that you scale by adding more power (CPU, RAM) to your existing machine.

Now vertical and horizontal scaling concepts can be applied to infrastructure as well as to any components and layers including databases. For example, Cassandra and MongoDB supports horizontal scaling out of the box. And MySQL - Amazon RDS (The cloud version of MySQL) provides an easy way to scale vertically by switching from small to bigger machines. One disadvantage in vertical scaling is that it involves downtime.

Comparing vertical to horizontal, it is obvious that horizontal is the choice if you don't want a downtime to your system or application. And vertical is the obvious choice if you want exceptional computing power in one of your application layer - database. Database is just an example. It could be a message queue or the app server container that would need scaling, and in this context, vertical scaling. It all depends on your architecture and your load prediction. These areas were covered in capacity planning or sizing plans in traditional data center model.

## Auto Scaling in AWS:

One of the prime reasons for businesses to embrace cloud is that it gives the agility to scale and compete more effectively. And while scaling adds complexity to the infrastructure, it adds agility and gives cost advantage for the product owner. Scaling without the use of AWS is slightly difficult but as Dan Brown says, 'Anything is possible. The impossible just takes longer."

Auto Scaling in AWS helps you maintain application availability and allows you to scale your Amazon EC2 capacity up or down automatically according to conditions you define. You can use Auto Scaling to help ensure that you are running your desired number of Amazon EC2 instances. Auto Scaling can also automatically increase the number of Amazon EC2 instances during demand spikes to maintain performance and decrease capacity during lulls to reduce costs. Auto Scaling is well suited both to applications that have stable demand patterns or that experience hourly, daily, or weekly variability in usage.

Whether you are running one Amazon EC2 instance or thousands, you can use Auto Scaling to detect impaired Amazon EC2 instances and unhealthy applications, and replace the instances without your intervention. This ensures that your application is getting the compute capacity that you expect.

Auto Scaling enables you to follow the demand curve for your applications closely, reducing the need to manually provision Amazon EC2 capacity in advance. For example, you can set a condition to add new Amazon EC2 instances in increments to the Auto Scaling group when the average utilization of your Amazon EC2 fleet is high; and similarly, you can set a condition to remove instances in the same increments when CPU utilization is low. If you have predictable load changes, you can set a schedule through Auto Scaling to plan your scaling activities. You can use Amazon Cloud Watch to send alarms to trigger scaling activities and Elastic Load Balancing to help distribute traffic to your instances within Auto Scaling groups. Auto Scaling enables you to run your Amazon EC2 fleet at optimal utilization.

Whenever you plan to use Auto Scaling, you must use certain building blocks to get started. This tutorial walks you through the process for setting up the basic infrastructure for Auto Scaling.

The following step-by-step instructions help you create a template that defines your EC2 instances, create an Auto Scaling group to maintain the healthy number of instances at all times, and optionally delete this basic Auto Scaling infrastructure. This tutorial assumes that you are familiar with launching EC2 instances and have already created a key pair and a security group.

**Tasks:**

Step 1: Create a Launch Configuration
Step 2: Create an Auto Scaling Group
Step 3: Verify Your Auto Scaling Group
Step 4: (Optional) Delete Your Auto Scaling Infrastructure

You may refer to AWS online documentation for further exploring the tasks to get auto scaling setup in AWS.

I want to iterate again that the book is only a direction for you to get your idea from a conceptual phase to production phase and the book guides you in that in every step.

In any of the chapter and in any of the section, if you feel there is less content that cover it end-to-end, no doubts, it is intended by the author. The author's objective is not to cover any concepts or ideas in depth but to give you the breadth of product engineering from infrastructure perspective. As an avid reader of technical books, author himself has read books that goes on with pages and pages of data about some things that would not matter much for anyone and with ever changing product landscape, your best bet as a reader to get more details on anything that the book covers will be to go online and search that respective product documentation. In our context, it is AWS product tutorial that you can refer for additional information.

## Disaster Recovery Concepts:

What is a disaster? Answer: Any event that has a negative impact on your business continuity or finances could be termed a disaster.

And disaster recovery is the practice of exercising business continuity plans (BCP) in real world and in real time.

First of all did you know that AWS has a products page and a separate solutions page to differentiate AWS products from services? Here we go with the URLs:

Solutions: http://bit.ly/aws-solutions-1
Products: http://bit.ly/aws-products-1

**Fun fact 1:** With frequent mentioning on AWS in this book, it's easy to think that the author is an AWS fan boy but that's not the case in reality. The author just picked AWS as the reference architecture for cloud because of its near-to-perfect IaaS capabilities in today's world of automation. Hello! Is Google listening? Visionary, missionary and actionary CEO (yes, actionary is a new word just invented), Sundar Pichai of Google surely sees future in the Google Cloud Products. But he and the other visionaries at Google seems not as bothered in the previous years. Pichai confesses that they have been doing cloud but mostly internally.

Interesting Read:

http://bit.ly/tehverge-interesting-topic

Considering all the above information, Disaster recovery around cloud needs to tackled in a slightly different way than it is tacked in conventional on premises data center.

**DR Exercises:**

On AWS, there are multiple ways you can architect disaster recovery. Yes, that must be obvious with AWS's strong cloud portfolio (in Liam Neeson's voice).

Recovery Time Objective (RTO) and Recovery Point Objective (RPO) are two of the most commonly used industry terms when building your DR strategy.

**Fun fact 2:** Microsoft however is surely in the race taking closest second place with Satya Nadella refactoring Microsoft as a cloud-first corporation. Red Hat OpenShift of course, is our reference architecture for PaaS and the fact is that OpenShift is built on top of AWS IaaS.

Okay, let's get back to topic. Why I mentioned about products and solutions separately is because, of course, AWS has a DR solution built in as an offering.

And off late Disaster Recovery as a Service (DRaaS) is gaining traction in the industry. DRaaS is the replication and hosting of physical or virtual servers by a third-party to provide failover in the event of a man-made or natural catastrophe.

Typically, DRaaS requirements and expectations are documented in a service-level agreement (SLA) and the third-party vendor provides failover to a different region of computing environment such as AWS either through a contract or pay-per-use basis. In the event of an actual disaster, an offsite vendor will be less likely than the enterprise itself to suffer the direct and immediate effects, allowing the provider to implement the disaster recovery plan even in the event of the worst-case scenario: a total or near-total shutdown of the affected enterprise.

DRaaS can be especially useful for small to mid-size businesses that lack the necessary expertise to provision, configure and test an effective disaster recovery plan (DRP). Using DRaaS also means the organization doesn't have to invest in -- and maintain -- their own off-site DR environment. An additional benefit is that DRaaS contracts can be flexible as the business' needs change. The downside, of course, is that the business must trust that the DRaaS service provider can implement the plan in the event of a disaster and meet the defined recovery time and recovery point objectives.

AWS, or on any platform, DR architect has the flexibility to choose the right approach that fits organization budget. The approaches could be as minimum as backup and restore from the cloud or full-scale multi-site solution deployed in onsite and AWS with data replication and mirroring. For our exercise, however we take an all cloud, all AWS solution. You may also consider multi cloud solution with AWS as primary and OpenShift or Rackspace® as secondary. Interestingly, that will become an even more robust solution.

Going by the saying, if we can't do an unit of work/task in say, 1 hour, or at least if we cannot figure out we can do it in relatively lesser time, then we are not doing it right. This is an original phrase that Mahesh M, the product innovation architect at Intellect Design Arena, Inc., usually says in every sprint and coincidentally this is something that holds very true for a DR exercise as well. When the catastrophe hits, all that you want to ensure is that the application's or the product's DR plan is working as expected. Visionary leader at Intellect, Nilesh Dambe, would nod his head in alignment and he would not or any other product owner would not disagree to test DR in real time and over time, once in a year, at least to make sure DR architecture is not outdated.

Fun fact: The aforementioned concept of getting it done in shorted time is actually a variant of Kanban. Kanban is a method for managing knowledge work with an emphasis on just-in-time delivery while not overloading the team members. This approach presents all participants with a full view of the process from task definition to delivery to a customer. Team members pull work from a queue.

Kanban in the context of software development can mean a visual process-management system that tells what to produce, when to produce it, and how much to produce - inspired by the Toyota Production System (TPS) and by Lean manufacturing. TPS is grounded on 2 main conceptual pillars:

a) Just-in-time - that means "Making only what is needed, only when it is needed, and only in the amount that is needed"
b) Jidoka - (Autonomation) that means "Automation with a human touch"

**Summary:**

This chapter dealt about scaling concepts,

vertical and horizontal scaling, auto scaling in AWS, disaster recovery concepts and disaster recovery setups in AWS.

Also covered broader topics such as Disaster Recovery as a Service (DRaaS) for a quick view on out of the box DR solutions.

There is a white paper on using AWS for Disaster Recovery written by AWS evangelist Jeff Barr on AWS blog site. DR on AWS brings in elasticity and brings back the state of the application rather than just the data. It is often considered difficult to bring back the state of the application itself than the data during a catastrophe and proper DR architecting helps in solving this problem to a greater extent.

# 6

## CONTINUOUS INTEGRATION, CONTINUOUS DEPLOYMENT AND CONTINUOUS DELIVERY

When you write software products, isn't one of your primary goal to reduce the cycle time between your idea and your actual usable software? By actual usable software, I meant your actual production version rather than your minimum viable product. I believe, most of you would say 'yes' to that question. Yes, we all want to reduce the build-test-deploy release life cycle to be short and disciplined. Not if daily deliveries, at the least bi-weekly releases, is what most of the product owners want, so dearly. Continuous Integration and Continuous Delivery is that practice that builds the culture of frequent, reliable deliveries.

By definition, Continuous Integration (CI) is a

development practice that requires developers to integrate code into a shared repository several times a day. Each check-in is then verified by an automated build, allowing teams to detect problems early.

Continuous delivery (CD) is a software engineering approach in which teams produce software in short cycles, ensuring that the software can be reliably released at any time. Continuous Delivery doesn't mean every change is deployed to production ASAP. It means every change is proven to be deployable at any time.

And CI/CD is the early seed of the DevOps movement that is currently adopted in the industry as the success factor for any enterprise grade product. DevOps is the clipped compound of "development" and "operations"). In other words, DevOps is the blending of tasks performed by a company's application development and systems operations teams. And CI /CD are one that makes the crux of DevOps. Continuous Integration and Continuous Delivery is the central theme of DevOps and almost everything related to DevOps is continuous. Continuous integration, continuous deployment, continuous delivery, continuous testing and many more.

Having gone through Continuous Integration and Continuous Delivery, you might be wondering what differentiate the above from Continuous

Deployment. Continuous deployment is the further step to continuous delivery, where we are not only steadily creating a deployable package, but as well deploying it steadily in real time.

Continuous deployment not necessarily means deploying to production immediately after CI and CD. Some of the full blown DevOps organizations such as Etsy, Flickr and Facebook do deploy to production several times a day, which is a great goal to work towards for companies that cater to billion customers, but it is not an absolute requirement and may even be counterproductive for some business which requires more process alignment before deliveries. This of course should have a proper regression in line to ensure that existing functionality does not break.

Right now the thought goes from theories to practices. How do we put this CI/CD/CD to practice? The answer is, in order to have a successful continuous deployment pipeline, you will definitely need some automated tools, but your success will not be directly dependent on exactly which tool you use, and you can use a single tool to automate and implement CI / $CD^2$ or you can use a combination of tools. Reference architecture for Continuous integration is of course possible to implement just by using Jenkins®.

**Fun fact:** It's often possible to put DevOps into an agile conversation, but remember that

DevOps and Agile are 2 different manifestos or philosophies and 'All things DevOps are not agile and all things Agile are not agile'. Some things DevOps can be Agile. However, as a practitioner of Agile for a long time, I understand that Agile is not the best (of course Waterfall is legacy and is not the best). But then what is the best for an application that runs from cloud? That's a complex piece of puzzle but to understand that lets understand some concepts of Agile. For Agile, code is the central piece. 2 of the Agile Manifesto Principles are:

a) Working software is the primary measure of progress and
b) Business people and developers must work together daily throughout the project.

In an agile environment, it's all iterative which is good, but what is bad is that agile treats software as just code. But in reality software is not just code. Software development is not pure coding, testing, engineering, architecture, infrastructure, management or design. It is cross-disciplinary.

From my understanding of a pro-agile-software-ecosystem, software products must be developed with user in the center. User is the king; End-User is the king and not the code. To get this done, speed matters and it's DevOps and not agile that matters a lot in speed to production.

## Popular Tools:

## Jenkins:

You can check-out any time you like, but you can never leave! – Famous lines from Eagles' Hotel California stand true for Jenkins continuous integration automation tool. Jenkins supports almost all types of source code management (SCM) repositories. That's a blessing. But when you upgrade your Jenkins platform and /or when you upgrade Jenkins plug-ins, most of the times there are issues that crop in and there are times the build won't just run. I personally have faced Maven build issues multiple times and I had to either downgrade Jenkins platform or downgrade the plug in itself, (or at times upgrade), or sometimes even had to fix IPV6 or had to go ahead with underlying host reboot. After a few occurrences of such issues, one would normally look for an alternate tool to switch to. Team city is one thing I have seen that takes place as a Jenkins alternative. But wait a minute. Even with all these issues (that are resolvable with enough research and community support), Jenkins stands tall in the field of CI. And it remains open source and free. Jenkins 2.0 comes with Cod Pipeline support as well.

Now let us look into some background information on Jenkins. Jenkins is an open source continuous integration tool written in Java. The project was forked from Hudson after a dispute with Oracle.

Jenkins provides continuous integration services for software development. It is a server-based system running in a servlet container such as Apache Tomcat. It supports SCM tools including AccuRev, CVS, Subversion, Git, Mercurial, Perforce, Clearcase and RTC. Jenkins can execute Apache Ant and Apache Maven based projects as well as arbitrary shell scripts and Windows batch commands. The primary developer and founder of Jenkins is Kohsuke Kawaguchi. Released under the MIT License, Jenkins is free software. Kawaguchi currently works as CTO at CloudBees. CloudBees is a provider of continuous delivery solutions powered by Jenkins CI. I see a lot of potential in this $50 million venture financed enterprise (Enterprise Jenkins).

Jenkins URL:       http://bit.ly/jenkins-ci-tool

CloudBees URL:   http://bit.ly/cloudbees

In Jenkins, builds can be started by various means, including being triggered by commit in a version control system, by scheduling via a cron-like mechanism, by building when other builds have completed, and by requesting a specific build URL. Jenkins is regarded as a better alternative to Thought Works' Cruise Control.

Even with all these suited up figure, Jenkins, deep inside are just a job scheduler and executor.

**Team city:**

TeamCity is a Java-based build management and continuous integration server from JetBrains. It was first released on October 2, 2006.[1] T

TeamCity is commercial software and licensed under a proprietary license. A Freemium license for up to 20 build configurations and 3 free Build Agent licenses are available. Open Source projects can request a free license.

There are a lot of good reasons to choose TeamCity. The product is very well documented and there are a lot of examples and tutorials available. Out on the Internet, there are many postings ranging from setting up basic CI with TeamCity to advanced topics such as using TeamCity's built-in NUnit test runner.

Some other reasons to choose TeamCity include:

i) Easy to setup, use, and configure
ii) Widely-used and well documented
iii) Integration with a wide variety of tools and technologies
iv) Professional Server is free for up to 20 build configurations.

Note that you can run as many instances of Professional Edition Server as needed. Larger organizations may require the purchase of the Enterprise Server version.

## CIaaS:

With the cloud advent, it seems like every business opportunity is transformed into some kind of 'as a service' form and Continuous Integration as a Service (CIaaS) came as a no surprise having seen IaaS to PaaS to SaaS to DRaaS.

## Code Pipeline:

Continuous Delivery is sometimes confused with Continuous testing. But both of these are 2 different entities. Continuous Delivery does not require testing (but it helps). It refers to the fact that the things you build on a regular basis could be shipped to the customer if needed. That's what Steve Jobs has said – 'Real artists' ship'. Now coming to the idea of Code pipeline, there are 2 commercial products out there with the same name:

a) AWS Code Pipeline
b) Jenkins – Pipeline as Code with Jenkins

However, by code pipeline, what is implied is

the generic concept of pushing the same code through the pipeline of delivery. This concepts contrasts from 'Infrastructure as a code', which involves writing code to manage continuous integration or to manage continuous delivery.

## Infrastructure as code (IaC):

Infrastructure as Code (IaC) is the process of managing and provisioning computing infrastructure (processes, bare-metal servers, virtual servers, etc.) and their configuration through machine-process able definition files, rather than physical hardware configuration or the use of interactive configuration tools.

There are many tools that fulfill infrastructure automation capabilities and utilize Infrastructure as Code. All Continuous Configuration Automation (CCA) tools can be thought of as an extension of traditional IaC frameworks; it leverages IaC to change, configure, and automate infrastructure, but also provides visibility, efficiency and flexibility in how your infrastructure is managed. These additional attributes provide enterprise level security and compliance - making companies keen on implementing these types of tools.

Continuous Configuration Automation (CCA) – Is the methodology or process of automating the deployment and configuration of settings and software for infrastructure both physical and virtual. Notable CCA tools are listed in the following table:

| Tool Name | Released by | Method | Approach |
| --- | --- | --- | --- |
| Ansible Tower | Ansible | Push | Declarative & Imperative |
| CFEngine | CFEngine | Pull | Declarative |
| Chef | Chef | Pull | Imperative |
| Otter | Inedo | Push | Declarative & Imperative |
| Puppet | Puppet | Pull | Declarative |
| SaltStack | SaltStack | Push | Declarative & Imperative |

Infrastructure as Code can be a key attribute of enabling best practices in DevOps – Developers become more involved in defining configuration and Ops teams get involved earlier in the development process. Tools that utilize IaC bring visibility to the state and configuration of servers and ultimately provide the visibility to users within the enterprise, aiming to bring teams together to maximize their efforts. Automation in general aims to takes the confusion and error-prone aspect of manual processes and makes it more efficient, and productive. Allowing for better software and applications to be created with flexibility, less downtime, and an overall cost effective way for the company. IaC is intended to reduce the complexity that kills efficiency out of manual configuration. Automation and collaboration are considered central points in DevOps; Infrastructure automation tools are often included as components of a DevOps tool chain.

## Summary:

This chapter answered few questions such as what exactly is CI/CD, Why do we need it. What are some of the industry standard tools? What is code pipeline? What is infrastructure as a code and tools to achieve it? Based on these answers, you should have enough ideas to proceed to the next chapter which majorly looks at another important concept named as 'Containerization'.

# 7

## QUICK INTRODUCTION TO DOCKER AND CONTAINERIZATION

Containerization has gained grounds again with the popularity of Docker, the open source containerization tool. It's an older concept with proven implementations in Linux landscape; however it only got its deserved importance since 2013, thanks to Docker.

To understand containerization it is important to understand virtualization. Virtualization, majorly OS level virtualization is a method in which the kernel of an OS can be shared in such a way that, instead of a single user-space instance or resource allocation, multiple user-space instances can be done which gives each user-space an allotted resource from the underlying hardware.

Hypervisors such as ESXi, Xen or KVM using which Windows or Linux or any other OS can be run is an example of virtualization implementation.

Containerization is an extra level of virtualization that goes on top of OS virtualization. For understanding purposes, it can be visualized as application virtualization.

Disclaimer: Containerization does not necessarily need to be on top of OS virtualization. It can be implemented on its own in a dedicated hardware.

Docker is a containerization tool that helps in achieving this application virtualization. Docker helps in running application in containers. Resource isolation features of Linux kernel is used in Docker which is the same as in CGroups and kernel namespace. That allows independent containers to run within a single Linux instance and thus avoiding the overhead of starting and maintaining virtual machines.

The reason Docker is introduced here is to use it for the purpose of architecting the product that we build in such a way that it can be packaged in a single Docker Image and ship that image for the purpose of running it on any platform. Prior to Docker, it required a lot of pre-requisite software layers or software stack to be installed prior to the deployment and prior to getting the product spin up in any environment, be it development instance, staging or even in production. With Docker, those pre requisite steps are cut down to just 2 steps.

Step 1: Get the Docker platform installed on the environment or laptop where the product will be running

Step 2: Get the Docker Image for the application/product, and simply run the Image to spin up the application in the form of containers.

Now having said that, life is not simple with Docker, it requires a lot of orchestration and monitoring to have it seamlessly run.

**Summary:**

This chapter is not even the tip of the ice berg but just an introduction that there is an ice berg that was broken from a much bigger glacier. Glacier here is the containerization concept and Iceberg the Docker tool.

References:

http://bit.ly/docker-tool
http://bit.ly/docker-tool-osx

# 8

## APPLICATION SETUP ON OPENSHIFT

I recollect a friend about YouTube channels that gone are the days of reading up a technical book for learning something new. For anything new or for anything that need hands-on he swipes to his YouTube channels on his Android phone (well, you guessed it right; he is an Android fan boy). Well, yes that is precisely correct with me and most of us and can't deny the fact that we do look at videos when we want to learn something new or want references for hands on stuff. But there is one thing that the videos cannot replace even with the 'pause' button on YouTube, and that is 'the continuity' and the beauty of re-reading when you don't understand something correctly. This book is not for those who are looking for a perfect text bookish type material but is for those who are part-YouTube-watchers and part-reference-book-seekers like me, I.

Well, now getting into business, let us look at what exactly is OpenShift, and of course that helps us understand about what could be a perfect Platform-as-a-service looks like. It is a well known fact that to understand 'something' well, a case study acts as a sharper tool than a philosophical description of that 'something' that we want to understand or learn. And thus there is no other perfect solution than the OpenShift platform to better understand what a Platform-as-a-service is. Okay, so Red Hat OpenShift is a Platform-as-a-Service that allows developers to deploy and run their applications on a real world public cloud. When we say Platform, it's as simple as 'a Tomcat 8 environment with JEE 8 running on a RHEL 7.2 on a 2 Core 4 Gig VM' and can be as 'complex as an array of Tomcat servers packaged on different type of VMs and put together with a backed data source in a clustered manner'. So it is basically an application platform that is ready made and can be spinned up in a few minutes and is only a few clicks away, no matter if it is the dev environment, staging environment or even the production environment. OpenShift is built on top of Docker Containers and Kubernetes Cluster Management and the entire OpenShift platform runs on Red Hat Enterprise Linux atop Amazon Web Services. And don't get confused that it's just for Tomcat or for Java. In their product video, Red Hat clearly mentions that OpenShift speaks your language.

And the supported languages are Ruby, PHP, Python, and JavaScript and well of course Java among the top list. There are other languages, middleware and databases supported by OpenShift and for a complete list, please visit their website: https://www.openshift.com

With AWS, which is primarily an Infrastructure as a Service platform, you need to create and provision EC2 Instances and install the required packages to create an application platform before you deploy. But with OpenShift, you are all set with the underlying infrastructure, and all that you have to do is to choose the required platform and it is ready for deployments. An equivalent PaaS environment in AWS is the AWS Elastic Beanstalk which is pretty much comparable with OpenShift. But there is more to OpenShift than Beanstalk and that is why OpenShift is more popular in the market. One such feature is the ability to run your own OpenShift environment on your on premises environment and thereby setting up a private cloud.

OpenShift comes in 3 flavors. OpenShift Online (Next Gen) which is a public PaaS, Red Hat OpenShift Container Platform 3.3 (Previously known as OpenShift Enterprise) and Red Hat OpenShift Dedicated.

OpenShift website clearly mentions that OpenShift Online has been completely rewritten recently to enable us to rapidly build and deploy Docker images and manage them on a robust, scalable platform. OpenShift Container Platform 3.3 is the enterprise grade container platform based on Docker and Kubernetes. More about this can be read on 'OpenShift for Developers: A Guide for Impatient Beginners' written by Grant Shipley and Graham Dumpleton. Available for purchase at http://bit.ly/openshift-for-developers-book.

OpenShift Dedicated is the 3$^{rd}$ flavor of OpenShift, which is basically your own OpenShift 3 cluster, securely connected to your internal network and backed by the experience of Red Hat Engineering, Operations, and Support.

Now creating an application on Tomcat can be well understood in the steps described in the developer's reference at http://bit.ly/tomcat-app

The steps basically includes, signing up with OpenShift, choosing an application platform (Tomcat 7 or 8 in this case), and running RHC commands to create and deploy Tomcat platform, and finally accessing the public URL and hooking up the codebase on Git. Deployments and configurations follow the initial setup.

**Summary:**

This chapter gave a brief about a real world

PaaS environment and that is Red Hat's OpenShift. Some basic ideas are described and web URLs to setting up a skeleton Tomcat application is referenced for getting hand-on with OpenShift.

# 9

## DEVOPS, NO OPS AND SUPPORT

IT has always been a business driven industry. However the modern economy requires IT shops, Product Companies and other Software organizations to quickly and evenly adapt to business in a more than ever agility and it is the DevOps and Cloud practice that helps these organization achieve such speed and agility.

Dev Ops simply means Development and Operations. In the recent times the shift has drifted more towards No-Ops from Dev Ops. No Ops basically means a completely automated Dev Ops practice. Or in other words, an obsessive compulsive automation. The word 'automation' is a repetitive word from the past (in the IT industry) and Dev Ops is the present buzz word. But the future is of course No Ops with more of Alexa driven DevOps and AI based platforms for Dev

Ops, for example.

DevOps brings in lot of good by products into the silos of product development, and some of such by products are 'less internal bureaucracies', 'sharper focus on results' and thereby, of course a better product and thus better customer satisfaction. It is spoken that more innovation projects are happening at the DevOps side (and the Data side) than on the hard core product development team at most of the product organizations these days because of the need for agility and a 100% fault tolerant, horizontally scalable, DR proof products.

With CI and CD in place, the calibration is ever more than any time in the industry and the interesting part is that Information Security compliance are not comprised a bit. In turn, with Intrusion Detection System (IDS) for the cloud standards, DevOps gets more functional.

Another important practice related to DevOps is the design and implementation of Micro services. It is a new world design approach to build an application as a set of small and independent services. The interlinking of services is primarily done through APIs and through REST based Web Services. Micro services can be written and deployed as a single or a group of services.

DevOps is based on repeat and revise principle.

When standardized patterns are used in a repetitive way to scale or to make environment fault tolerant, Infrastructure as Code comes into play, and Infrastructure as Code is a very powerful medium that aligns with DevOps principles. It is a practice in which infrastructure is provisioned and managed using code and software development techniques, such as version control and continuous integration.

Configuration Management and Policy Management are other areas of DevOps. Application Performance Monitoring and Log monitoring also are components of DevOps and it helps in mitigating problems and in providing production support in an awesome way. Communication and collaboration tools also come under the radar of DevOps and so are the innovation area of infrastructure for Data Analytics and Data mining along with AI based bots infrastructure.

When it comes to configuration managements, there are few top names such as Chef, Puppet, Ansible, SaltStack, Docker, Mesosphere and Habitat. The usual evaluations revolve around those tools and we have to find the tool that fits the best for our use cases and what's usually seen is not a single tool but multiple of these tools works in conjunction and solves different purposes. For example, a usual comparison is between Chef's new Habitat tool and Docker. Does Habitat work well with Docker? If yes, what problem does

Habitat solve or is it yet another tool to replace Docker ecosystem such as Docker Swarm, Docker Machine and Docker Compose? Well the answer to that is, Docker and Habitat does not really overlap much. Docker is a tool to run processes inside a bunch of Linux security mechanisms collectively called as a 'container'. Whereas Habitat acts as a tiny stub that wraps around the processes to handle things like runtime configuration distribution, secrets data transfer, and service discovery. In short, when deployed in the correct way, Docker and Habitat collaborate to solve uses cases that cannot be solved with only Docker or only Habitat. A good analogy to it is the way car braking assistance technology ABS and EBD works together to come up with the safest braking mechanism. ABS stands for Anti-Lock Braking System which prevents wheels from locking during emergency braking. EBD stands for Electronic Brake Force Distribution System distributes braking forces to wheels that are carrying more of the load and less to those that are doing less work and thus achieving the best and lowest stopping distance without causing accidents or lowering the impact. Now we can't say that just having ABS and EBD is enough, we also need curtain air bags, steering assist and various other safety mechanisms to make the automobile safest as possible. The same goes with infrastructure and tools such as Docker, Habitat and many other such infrastructure tools.

I love analogies and I just cannot get past it here by comparing these tool sets with America's most off road worthy trucks. A Toyota Tacoma TRD Pro or a Jeep Wrangler Rubicon Hard Rock, or a 'bring it on', Raptor. It would be an easiest and an apt choice for that next Alaskan adventure in the snowy mountains or that muddy off road trail to choose that TRD Pro or that Jeep. But would both of these trucks can with stand the conditions of a Baja Sandy ride or a Rocky Crawl like the Raptor do? Answer is Yes and the answer is also No. What does that mean? There is no tool that is the best choice for everything but there is a tool that is the best choice for specific use cases. That is similar to saying Mesosphere and Kubernetes can form the basis of infrastructure automation but without Docker we are going nowhere in real world scalability and security. But there are still things that are not doable with Docker. Going back to the analogy, like Raptor that is pretty wide to get past a narrow trail that the Jeep or Tacoma can easily do. All of these beasts give the power to do it, but it's the team or the men behind the wheels that makes it doable and so is the case with these toolsets and the team behind making it work for specific problems or use cases.

While considering application support, developers or operations or even support associates require a lot of log information, data and KPIs to solve or mitigate issues. Some of the awesome tools such as DynaTrace and

AppDynamics provide AWS or Azure account level log information from the servers using agent based active monitoring yet without administrator type access to any of the servers. This is a major area of focus for identifying issues and resolving problems without impact to the environment.

Last but not the least, NoOps (No Operations) is the concept that an IT environment can become so automated and abstracted from the underlying infrastructure that there is no need for a dedicated team to manage software in-house. PaaS platforms such as AppFog and Heroku describe their environment as NoOps platforms.

### Summary:

This chapter is all about introduction to DevOps principles and the areas that cover DevOps. It also gives a hint about No Ops and Support area of Product Engineering.

# 10

# SUMMARY

The book is a quick dive into cloud based product engineering and covers important aspects of standing up an application in the cloud using DevOps principles. AWS and OpenShift are briefly covered in this book to help the reader catch up speed on cloud engineering. The technology landscape change between the time I began writing book and the time I finished with it for publishing in itself is so vast that it makes it really a necessity to come up with a future revised version of this book without which the modern problems of product engineering for infrastructure cannot be solved. Some things goes backward to legacy and becomes history and some other things goes forward to create a benchmark in the industry to become the future and only a handful of techniques and technology make it to the time machine. That said, it's certain that most of the code we write to solve today's use cases will either obsolete or become legacies unless the code itself does machine learning and deep learning. Well, that makes it clear that AI is the future and it's a no brainer to explore more about it make any domain better equipped to adapt to changes. The way most tools makes entries are Anyways, Good luck with setting up your next big thing on your favorite cloud provider platform and good luck with that AI thing.

# AFTERWORD

There are numerous resources to help acquaint with the cloud concepts in product engineering. This book may look like just one of them. However the reason behind writing this book is to help those who are new to cloud based development such as those from legacy enterprise organizations which are slowly adapting to cloud and devops and this is also a quick reference for system architects and those who don't have a big picture about product engineering based on cloud concepts. Areas such as Docker, Kubernetes/Docker Swarm etc are still evolving and there would be rapid adaption of these containerization mechanism and container orchestration tools in the coming years. When industry is rapidly evolving, this book stands as a small contribution towards cloud readiness and cloud adaption.

# ABOUT THE AUTHOR

Ajith Joseph is a cloud solutions architect, devops advocate, viz. cloud evangelist and an infrastructure engineer with strong development background with over 10 years of experience in various aspects of product development and software services delivery. He has worked for mid-size to large Fortune 500 corporations and is currently employed with Intellect Design Arena, Inc., a product based fin-tech Company at Greater New York City area. At Intellect Design, he works for Intellect SEEC, an Exponential Insurance Products Company.

Ajith is an avid Java developer, an APM consultant, a system administrator and a solutions specialist as well. His personal favorites include Red Hat OpenShift - Platform as a Service, Amazon Web Services – Infrastructure as a Service (majorly), Java EE, Docker – Containerization Tool, Apache Commons – Set of Java APIs, Angular JS – HTML5 based JavaScript Framework for Single Page Applications, Selenium – Test Tool, and the last but not the least Jython – Scripting Language.

www.ingramcontent.com/pod-product-compliance
Lightning Source LLC
Chambersburg PA
CBHW071002050326
40689CB00014B/3462